This lively and entertaining book looks at the exciting world of animals, large and small.

Find out how porcupine fish defend themselves, why frogs have long, sticky tongues and how dolphins communicate with one another across the oceans.

Acknowledgments:
The publishers would like to thank Wendy Body for acting as reading level consultant and Chris Tydeman, who works for the World Wide Fund For Nature, for advising on scientific content.

Photographs by Ardea; front cover: Bruce Coleman.

Illustrations on pages 37 (bottom), 38 and 39 by Terry Gabbey.

Designed by Gaynor Berry.

British Library Cataloguing in Publication Data
Ganeri, Anita
    Animals.
    1. Animals
    I. Title   II. Allen, Graham
    591
    ISBN 0-7214-1195-9

First edition
Published by Ladybird Books Ltd Loughborough Leicestershire UK
Ladybird Books Inc Auburn Maine 04210 USA

Printed in England (3)

Animals

written by ANITA GANERI
illustrated by GRAHAM ALLEN

Ladybird Books

What are animals?

Did you know that there are probably more than ten million different kinds of animals on Earth? Animals come in a huge range of shapes, sizes and colours and they are found in almost every part of the world.

Polar bears, seals and snowy owls live in the frozen regions of the Arctic. They have thick fur or feathers to keep them warm.

Many types of animals live in the
Sahara desert. During the day they
usually shelter from the heat of the
sun in burrows.

Some animals can even live many
thousands of metres down in the sea,
where it is cold and dark.

Animals without backbones

Animals that do not have backbones to support their bodies are called **invertebrates**. Some, like worms, jellyfish and squid, have soft bodies. Others, like snails, crabs, sea urchins and insects, have hard shells or cases to protect them.

Coral reefs are made by millions of tiny sea invertebrates called coral polyps. These creatures attach themselves to rocks and build hard cases round their bodies. Many other invertebrates, such as anemones, giant clams, sea slugs, crabs and urchins live among the coral reefs.

Not all invertebrates live in water. Many slugs, snails, spiders, centipedes, millipedes, insects and worms live on dry land.

Insects

Insects are invertebrates that have a tough covering round their bodies. The covering is hinged so that the insect can move easily.

All insects have six legs, and most have wings and can fly. Beetles, butterflies, ants, grasshoppers and houseflies are all insects.

Insects have large **compound eyes**. Our eyes have only one lens to see through but a dragonfly has over 40,000 lenses in each eye.

A butterfly starts life as a tiny egg. This hatches into a caterpillar, which spends most of its time feeding.

The caterpillar then builds a hard case called a **cocoon** round itself.

Inside the cocoon, the caterpillar changes into an adult butterfly.

Fish

Fish, amphibians, reptiles, birds and mammals are all **vertebrates**. This means that they have backbones inside their bodies to support them. **Fish** are vertebrates that are

The most ferocious fish is the great white shark. It has huge jaws with rows of razor-sharp teeth. This shark sometimes attacks and kills people.

specially designed for living in
water. Their bodies are covered
in overlapping scales which are
often beautifully coloured.

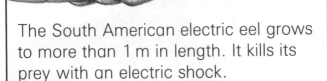

The South American electric eel grows
to more than 1 m in length. It kills its
prey with an electric shock.

The seahorse is a very
strange-looking
fish. Its tail
doesn't have fins
but is curled up
so that it can be
hooked round
weed or coral
to anchor the
seahorse.

Amphibians

Frogs, toads, salamanders and newts are **amphibians**. These unusual creatures can live in water and on land, but they must return to water to lay their eggs.

It is fairly easy to tell a frog from a toad. Frogs usually have damp, smooth skins and toads have dry, bumpy skins.

The amazing water-holding frog lives in the very dry Australian desert. Rain falls there only once every five or six years. Then the frog takes in so much water that it swells up like a balloon. It lives on this water until the next rainfall.

Frogs and toads have long, sticky tongues attached to the fronts of their mouths which they use to catch slugs, insects, worms and even birds. They blink and squeeze their eyes down on their food to help them to swallow.

Reptiles

Today's **reptiles** are the descendants of the dinosaurs which roamed the Earth over 65 million years ago. They include snakes, lizards, turtles, tortoises and crocodiles.

The chameleon is one of the few animals that can move each eye in a different direction at the same time.

The longest snake in the world is the reticulated python, which can grow up to 10 m long.

Reptiles have dry, scaly skins.
They lay their eggs on land,
often in nests dug
in soil or sand.

Cobras kill their prey
by injecting them
with poison using
two huge fangs.

Pythons have very elastic jaws which
they can open wide enough to swallow
large animals, such as sheep and pigs.
They swallow them whole!

Birds

Birds have horny beaks and their bodies are covered in feathers which keep them warm and dry. All birds have wings but not all of them can fly. The huge ostrich can run very fast instead and the penguin is an excellent swimmer.

Many birds build nests to lay their eggs in. The parents bring food back for the chicks until they are old enough to look after themselves.

Birds have different shaped beaks depending on what they eat.

Hummingbirds have long, thin beaks for sucking sweet **nectar** from deep inside flowers.

Hawks have sharp, hooked beaks for tearing meat apart.

Pelicans use their large, pouched beaks to scoop fish out of the water.

Mammals

There are over 4,000 different types of **mammals** in the world. They range from humans, whales and bats to elephants, rabbits and mice. All mammals have some hair or fur on their bodies.

Bats are the only mammals that can fly. Their wings are made of skin stretched between their front and back legs.

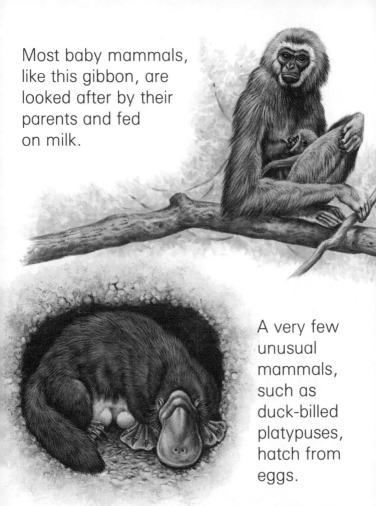

Most baby mammals, like this gibbon, are looked after by their parents and fed on milk.

A very few unusual mammals, such as duck-billed platypuses, hatch from eggs.

The sloth is the slowest mammal, with a top speed of only 1 km per hour. It spends eighteen hours a day fast asleep.

Feeding

All animals must eat to stay alive. Some animals feed on plant leaves, stems and nectar. These animals are called **herbivores**.

Koalas will eat the leaves of only one tree — the eucalyptus.

The blue whale has a gigantic appetite. Every day it eats as much as 4 tonnes of tiny sea creatures called **plankton**.

Meat-eating animals are called **carnivores**. They have to chase or trap their prey.

Spiders trap flying insects in webs which they spin from silk thread.

Lions hunt in groups to share the work. Often it is the lionesses that catch the prey.

Tricks with colour

Animals use colours in different ways. Some have coats or skins which blend in with where they live. This is called **camouflage**. It hides them from enemies and lets them hunt for food without being seen easily.

The praying mantis larva looks just like the bark of a tree.

Colour is also used to send out messages to other animals. Bright reds and yellows often warn that an animal is poisonous or has a nasty bite or sting.

The poison in this tree frog's skin can kill a monkey.

Many male birds, such as this peacock, show off their bright colours to attract a mate.

Protection from danger

Animals protect themselves from danger in many ways. Some have tough, leathery skins or hard shells and scales. Others are covered in sharp quills or prickles.

If a porcupine fish is attacked, it gulps in water and blows itself up so that it is too big to swallow. The spines on its body also stick out for extra protection.

This owl butterfly has huge **eyespots** on its wings. It flashes these to frighten away animals that attack it.

Some animals have special survival tricks. A lizard's tail may break off if it is grabbed so that the lizard can escape. A new tail soon grows.

Some animals use strong smells to put off their enemies. The skunk turns its back on attackers, raises its tail and squirts a horrible-smelling liquid at them.

The scaly anteater – the pangolin – is protected by scales on its back. When it rolls itself into a ball it is safe from attack.

How animals move

Most animals need to move to find food or a mate, or to escape from danger.

Many have special features, such as fins, wings and flippers, to help them.

Many monkeys and other tree-top animals have long arms for swinging through the branches.

The bird in flight glides on huge outstretched wings.

Some animals are great jumpers. Red kangaroos can bound along the ground at high speed, covering over 10 m in one jump.

Some animals move very slowly. It would take a garden snail nearly eight days to travel just 1 km.

27

Animal homes

Many animals move from place to place in search of food, so they do not need a home. Others need a safe place to lay their eggs, bring up their young and sleep. Animals may live in their homes all year round, or use them just for a short time to look after their young.

Harvest mice build summer nests in cornfields and hedges.

Tiny insects called termites build huge mounds out of mud, sand and spit. A mound may be up to 12 m tall and contain over ten million termites. Inside is a maze of tunnels leading to rooms where food is stored or the termite eggs hatch.

TERMITE NEST

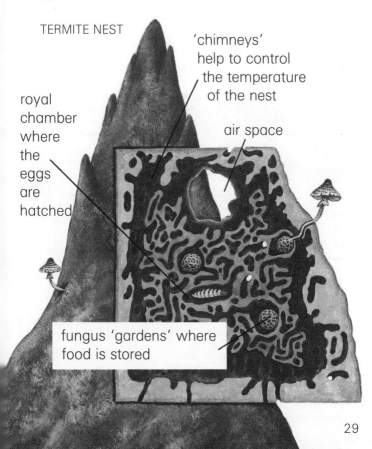

'chimneys' help to control the temperature of the nest

air space

royal chamber where the eggs are hatched

fungus 'gardens' where food is stored

Finding a mate

Animals have all kinds of ways of attracting a mate so that they can have a family. Male birds dance or show off their bright colours. Animals such as frogs and crickets use special mating calls.

Male bowerbirds build arches from grass or straw, which they decorate with brightly-coloured shells, feathers and flowers to attract a female.

Animals that come out at night use special smells and signals to attract mates. Male fireflies glow very brightly so that females can see them in the dark.

When she is ready to mate, an Indian moon moth gives off a strong scent. This can attract a male moth from over 10 km away.

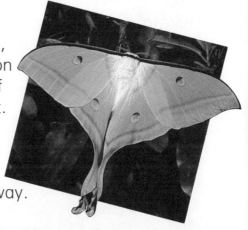

Some males, like these deer, fight to try and impress the females.

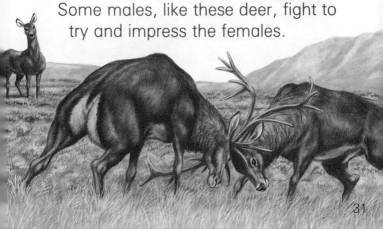

Animal babies

Some baby animals never see their parents. Most fish lay their eggs underwater, then leave them to hatch by themselves. However, birds look after their young. They sit on their eggs to keep them warm and bring food for the chicks.

Baby scorpions ride on their mother's back until they are two weeks old.

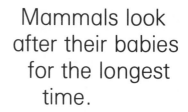

Mammals look after their babies for the longest time.

When a baby kangaroo, or joey, is born, it is only as big as a bee. It crawls into its mother's pouch and stays there for about six months, feeding on milk, and growing.

Ocean sunfish lay up to 3,000 million eggs at a time.

Animal talk

Animals cannot use words the way that people do. Instead they have special ways of calling their young, warning others of danger and showing their feelings. Some call to one another by croaking, barking and whistling.

Talkative crows can make over 300 different sounds.

Dolphins swim together in schools. They talk to one another by making chattering and whistling sounds.

When dogs growl and snarl and bristle their fur it means 'go away'.

Honey bees do a special honey dance to tell other bees where to find nectar and pollen.

Zoos and safari parks

In zoos and safari parks you can see animals from all over the world. Many of these are very rare in the wild.

Early zoos were quite cruel places, with animals kept in small cages.

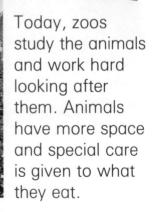

Today, zoos study the animals and work hard looking after them. Animals have more space and special care is given to what they eat.

THESE BABOONS HAVE A SPECIAL DIET AND MUST NOT BE FED BY THE PUBLIC

The Arabian oryx is the world's rarest antelope. In 1972 there were none left in the wild so the Phoenix Zoo in Arizona, USA, started breeding them.

The zoo was then able to send a herd of oryxes back to the wild.

An important part of a zoo's work is to teach people more about animals so that they can help to protect them.

Our pets

People have kept animals in their homes for thousands of years. Dogs were first trained to be working animals. They helped people to hunt for food and guarded their houses.

Dogs still work today, guiding blind people and helping the police and farmers.

Many people have pet cats, gerbils and fish. Some keep more unusual pets, such as snakes, spiders and even pumas! These animals are difficult to look after, though, because they need special food and care.

Puppies and kittens are popular pets. They need to be carefully looked after if they are to stay healthy and happy.

The ancient Egyptians kept cats as pets but they also worshipped them as gods. If a pet cat died, its owner shaved off his eyebrows as a sign of grief.

Animals in danger

Many of the world's animals are in danger of dying out for ever. Whales are hunted and killed for their meat, elephants for their tusks and leopards for their skin.

Blue whales have been killed to make oil, petfoods and glue so that now they are in danger of being destroyed altogether.

This puffin's feathers have been stuck together with oil spilt from a tanker at sea.

Many more types of animals die out when their forest homes are cut down or rivers and seas are **polluted** by chemicals and oil.

Conservation

Today, there are **conservation** groups all over the world working hard to help animals in danger. If we act quickly we may be able to save some of these rare creatures from becoming extinct.

Green turtles were once quite common in warm, tropical seas. But they were hunted for their meat, eggs and beautiful shells and are now very rare.

In the 1940s, there were about 100,000 tigers in the world. People killed tigers for their skin and destroyed their homes. By 1970, only about 4,000 were left. Operation Tiger, a project set up by the World Wide Fund For Nature, has helped to save the tigers and there are now about 8,000 in the wild.

Glossary of some words you need to know

amphibians Animals that can live both in water and on land.

birds Two-footed animals with feathers and wings.

camouflage The use of colour or patterns by a plant or animal in order for it to blend into its surroundings and make it difficult to see.

carnivores Animals (and sometimes plants) that feed on meat.

cocoon A case which a caterpillar forms about itself, in which it changes from a caterpillar to a butterfly.

conservation Saving and protecting the natural world.

compound eyes An eye made up of many separate lenses.

eyespots Coloured eyelike markings on the wings of some butterflies and moths.

fish Animals with scaly skins that live in water.

herbivores Animals that feed on plants.

invertebrates Animals that do not have backbones.

mammals Animals that have fur or hair and feed their babies milk.

nectar A sweet liquid made by some flowers.

plankton Tiny plants and animals that drift in water near the surface.

pollute To spoil or harm the natural world.

reptiles Animals such as lizards or snakes, with scaly, dry skin.

vertebrates Animals that have backbones.